YOUR LOGO HERE

Photographs From Southern California, 2004 – 2006
By Deanna Templeton, Text by Ed Templeton

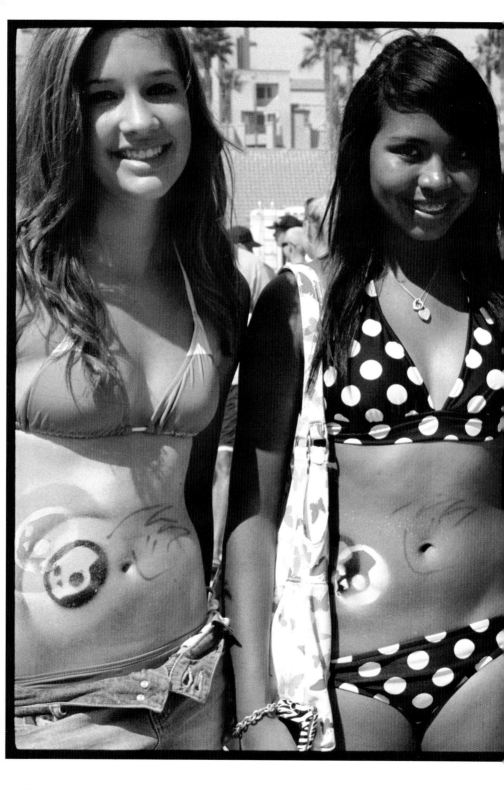

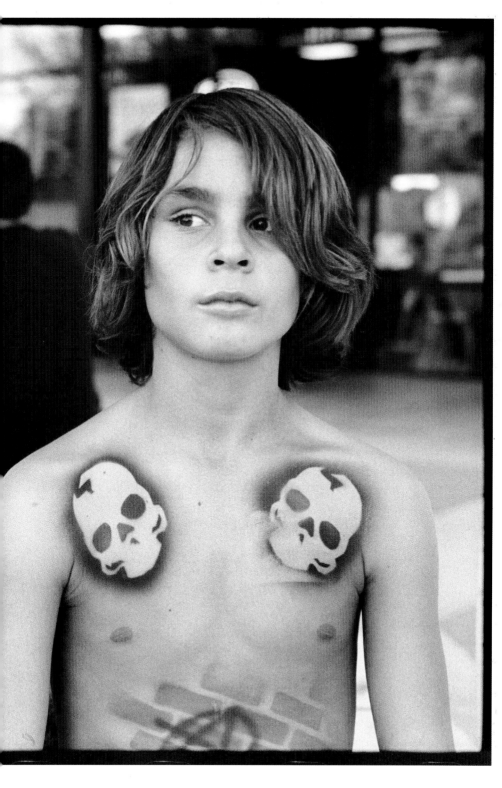

*W*hen I look at these photographs I see no judgment, just a simple show of what is going on. The subjects seem proud of the way they look and what they have done with their bodies. They smile and look like they are having fun. Not a care in the world. It is also pure marketing genius. For the cost of a few cans of spray paint and a stencil, these companies have scored a major coup in the battle for consumers' eyes feasting on their logos. What better place to land your company's logo than on the flesh of a young, healthy, 90% naked, 17 year old girl? You can pay over 30,000 dollars to have your ad in a magazine, or on a billboard hovering above the freeway and not get this sort of attention. I can safely say that all males ages 14-55 at the beach that day will see your logo. Add to that plenty of female views too. Many thinking, "Where can I get one of these sweet logos?" Either way, it gets viewed. Even now through the pages of this book, the companies win more eyes. They succeeded in turning portraits of beach going teenagers into advertisements. What are these girls getting paid for their valuable advertising real estate? Nothing. In fact, they are lining up to be the next walking billboard for "company X." I often wonder about this generation and the seemingly disappeared notion of selling out. It's a "get famous at whatever cost" mindset. Respect, reputation, and character are not seen as valuable. The lack of critical thinking in getting one of these spray-on logos is a perfect example. These girls are completely unaware that they are being used for their bodies. In fact they seem to see it the opposite way, like they are gaining something; a free piece of "body-art." The idea of becoming a corporate shill or a walking billboard is nonexistent. Some take it to the extreme and get completely covered with company logos, Honda Cars, for instance. They choose to become an ad, the very thing that most people view as an annoying reality of everyday life. Another aspect of this is the sexual play involved. There is a human element in the application of these logos, Someone is placing the stencil on the body and squirting a mist of paint through it onto the skin. Touch is part of the game. Having logos covering your body, or even autographs written on you by a local sports hero is all a glaring statement that you have been touched in all these places. It's a flirtatious thing to do at a time when you are discovering the power of your body. As an imaginary parent of one of these young girls I would recoil at the thought of my 14 year old daughter being fondled all over with paint and felt tipped marker. And do you know how hard spray paint is to scrub off? Well imagine your inner thighs, chest or upper back!

The people doing this are willing participants and they certainly have a right to do what they please with their time and their bodies. They don't have to listen to a curmudgeonly old man of 34 who is looking in from the outside and thinking about how silly kids are these days. Because for sure when I was 14 there were people looking at my actions in disbelief and befuddlement. I guess I need to have some kind of faith that these girls will look back and laugh. Or just dismiss it as no big whoop, just kids being kids. But in truth I worry. In Southern California we live in the shadow of Hollywood and get hit first with the barrage of lusciously tanned imagery of success through 6-pack abs and great hair. The way you look is everything, and the way you think is nothing. I can't help but think of a song lyric written by Eve Libertine of the band Crass: System, System, System, they'll teach her how to cook / Teach her how to look / They'll teach her all the tricks / Create another victim for their greasy pricks. / Poor little girly, poor little wench / Another little object to prod and pinch. / Poor little sweety, poor little filly, / They'll fuck her mind so they can fuck her silly.

I want to offer some sort of solution to this, because I hate when people just rant about a bunch of bad things and don't offer any ideas about how to solve them. Any mothers or fathers reading this, please take the time to teach your sons and daughters about critical thinking. Nobody seems to even ask the questions anymore, and nobody is held accountable. My grandfather put it to me this way: Man is not an island, you don't live in a vacuum. What you think, and say, and do interacts with others. Your name and your character, they are the most precious things you have, protect them at all costs.

What compelled Deanna Templeton to take these images? The lack of statement from her allows the viewer to form his/her own opinions. I instantly thought of corporate advertising and sexual politics, but what does another person see? What do females think? I feel very voyeuristic. My eyes naturally gravitate towards the logos and words emblazoned across their tummies, breasts and thighs, making me feel sort of creepy…

-and sort of like buying some skate-shoes. -ed templeton